Happiness
is a Choice

Happiness is a Choice

"So Why Not Make It?"

Ken Shankweiler

ISBN: 154262486X
ISBN 13: 9781542624862
Library of Congress Control Number: 2017900947
CreateSpace Independent Publishing Platform
North Charleston, South Carolina

Contents

*"I've learned that if you pursue
happiness, it will elude you. But if
you focus on your family, the needs
of others, your work, meeting new
people, and doing the very best you
can, happiness will find you."*

U̲N̲K̲N̲O̲W̲N̲!

Dedication!

I dedicate this book to the late KJ Shankweiler, who really exemplified the lessons found in this book, by always laughing, joking, making ridiculous remarks and gestures, even in the face of serious adversities in his life. His happiness was contagious!

I miss you son!

Thanks!

My GRATITUDE GOES out to my loving wife, Jet, and my son Jason for their love, support and encouragement during the years I spent writing this book. To my good friends, Rick Lieibley, Titus Pina, Ted Lerner, Kit Sumabat, Alex Cecilio, Randy Brown, and the many others I may have failed to mention here, for offering me their support and help with this endeavor.

To the CreateSpace Publishing arm of Amazon, especially Gaines Hill, I give my sincere thanks for the guidance and professional help!

To my Illustrator, Hamor Manahan, I offer my eternal gratitude for his artistic talents and contribution to this book. A true artist in every sense of the word!

And of course, to the many people I have met through my numerous speaking engagements, seminars, advisory sessions, consultations and through social interaction at many levels, I say thank you for always inspiring me and offering me so many of life's lessons, which I have shared in this book.

And lastly, I want to thank everyone whoever gave me a break in my life and career which allowed me to grow and succeed!

May God Bless All of You!

Foreword

BY THE AUTHOR

THIS IS SUCH an exciting time for me, as I have worked for many years on writing this book. The work feels so worthwhile and the reward, just for accomplishing a dream, is so great that it's hard to describe.

For much of my life, I have been called upon by others, for whatever reason, to share my opinions and thoughts about their lives and personal situations. I'm not so sure about how meaningful or valuable those opinions and thoughts may have been, but I have considered it a privilege to have been asked. In all of my responses, I have always tried to place a positive spin on the situation and try to get the person to walk away with some useful and happy ideas.

My life, like nearly everyone else's, has been a series of ups and downs. From a humble beginning in rural Pennsylvania, growing up in a very simple, but wonderful environment, with a strong, bull headed German mom and a quiet, dedicated, gentle step-dad, to reaching the top of the Corporate Ladder. It is amazing how life just buzzes by and then you look back and ask, "How did that happen?" So many events pass by us, as this thing called "life" marches on. In this book, I am hoping to share with you the more positive things that have influenced me and how I managed to use them to not only advance myself, but more importantly advance many of the people around me, particularly in the workplace.

If there is one really true lesson learned in all of this it is that we really need to stay focused on the present and future. There is absolutely nothing we can do about the past, so why waste time on it! I learned this the hard way, by beating myself up for years, trying to explain why some things went wrong. And then I finally realized it doesn't matter! It was at that moment that life dramatically changed for me, as my eyes opened up to what was and is directly in front of me, which is really all that matters.

Through this revelation I came to discover that I really possessed the main ingredients to the recipe of "Happiness". As I said earlier, I am excited about being able to share all of this with you, within the preceding pages of this book, and truly hope you will make your own discoveries and experience the same excitement as me.

One thing for sure, is that I have had my fair share of mistakes, failures, bad decisions, and all of that and I am not immune from a great deal of criticism from many who's paths have crossed mine throughout the many, many years I have lived on this earth. To them I say, "Sorry"! But I know there isn't a person alive who doesn't have critics, as that is just as much a part of life as everything else. But the true message here is that it doesn't really matter and if we want to achieve this great feeling called "happiness", we need to recognize that and let all those old feelings go. Remember, we can't change the past.

So in looking at where you and I are going, let's focus on the "life lesson's" I will be presenting to you in this book.

My true dream is that you will find something in this book, which will inspire you, enlighten you, or simply just lift you up! It is not my primary ambition to be a bestselling author, to make money from this book, nor to gain any fame, but to simply and hopefully offer something meaningful and rewarding to you the reader.

Enjoy reading and I hope to hear from you somewhere along the way!

God Bless!
Ken Shankweiler

CHAPTER 1

Introduction

What is Happiness?

"Happiness is when what you think, what you say, and what you do are in harmony."

—Mahatma Gandhi

It is important to remember that any discussion about a specific topic, such as this book, should always begin with a definition of the topic. First of all "Happiness" is a very broad based word and I'm sure that my readers will all have somewhat of a personal definition or sense of what "happiness" means. Therefore, it is important to differentiate between what makes you happy and what happiness is. Certainly, what makes me happy, may not make you happy in a great many instances. For example if I love a certain food and that food makes me incredibly happy and you don't like that particular food, we will not be in agreement at all on this trigger of happiness. But this is an example of how happiness is created or generated and we must remember to segregate the "definition" from "causes or effects".

So I would simply like to offer the definition(s) found in Webster's Dictionary as a basis for the use of the word throughout this book.

"Happiness" *Noun:* the state of being happy: an experience that makes you happy

Definition

> 1 : a state of well-being and contentment : joy
> 2 : a pleasurable or satisfying experience
> 3 : felicity, aptness

Synonyms: beatitude, blessedness, bliss, blissfulness, felicity, gladness, joy, warm fuzzies
Antonyms: calamity, ill-being, misery, sadness, unhappiness, wretchedness
First use: 15th century

For myself and without making the topic overly complicated, I find it simple to say that "happiness is feeling good inside"!

You Decide!

"No one can make you happy, except you. No one can make you feel or do anything, except you!"

— Dr Ken

One of the most unique and interesting things about the human brain, is its ability to think, make deductions, and apply logic. It is the main difference between man and all other animals. We look at our choices and decide what we want to do, or be, or feel, or try, or say, and a whole multitude of other things. Then we decide!

With that said, isn't it amazing that most people never come to realize that the way they feel at any given moment is entirely up to them? Your feelings, emotions, outlook are solely determined by your decision to feel that way. We have the control button and no one else can operate it. Yet many people keep pushing the wrong buttons and wonder why they are not getting the desired results. Understanding this concept of making a choice is what this book is all about.

Many people go through life blaming others for how they feel. In reality, the truth is you are the only one who can decide how you feel. So if that is the case, why don't more of us choose to be happy? Well, that's an interesting question. When I discuss attitudes in a later chapter, you will see that man is basically designed to be negative and if we don't learn about this negative influence, we may never learn how to be happy people.

No one can make you laugh, cry, smile, frown, get angry, or any of the other human emotions known to man. Only you can decide these things. As an example, if I say something really funny to you and you decide not to laugh, that's a decision you make. No matter what I do or say, you won't laugh, because you have decided not to laugh. If you have ever pulled this on a friend just for a joke, then you know exactly what I mean.

So it's a fact, no one else can make you happy, only you can. So why would anyone choose to be unhappy? Well, it's quite easy to understand if we take a closer look at the psychology of the problem, which is more clearly defined in a later chapter about attitudes. Our past experience and human nature guides us to want to blame someone or something else for creating our state of mind. We usually want to believe that some external source has created how we feel. But that simply isn't true! Under normal circumstances people make the final decision as to how they feel. Of course there is the exception of a physiological problem, such as a chemical imbalance, which takes this choice completely out of the hands of the individual. I am addressing those who are not physiologically impaired.

Of course, I am not suggesting to you that others don't have any influence on our feelings! They do, but only when we decide to let them do so. And there, lies one of the secrets to being happy. If you are aware of these influences, and you focus your energy on understanding them and knowing when they are in play, you can control your emotions and not necessarily let them have a negative impact on you. Happy people do this all of the time. They know how to be sympathetic, how to be understanding, and how to agree or disagree, without changing their own mood. So if we can determine when an outside influence, such as a family member, friend, colleague, the TV, etc., is delivering an unhappy message, then we can also determine how we want to feel about it, in the long run. Of course, this is much easier said than done!

Just recently an acquaintance of mine came up to me at a restaurant, while I was eating my lunch, and asked if he could join me for a few minutes. I invited him to sit down and after the customary greetings, he proceeded to tell me that he always notices that I look so happy whenever he sees me in public and he wishes he could feel that way. He then asked me if we could get together and discuss how I manage to be that way. I agreed and a few days, following this encounter, we sat down in his apartment over a cup of coffee and had a two hour discussion about happiness.

He proceeded to tell me about some very serious problems he was having and that no matter how hard he tries to think positive, he always winds up feeling depressed. He spoke a great deal about his problems and I tried my best to be a good listener, which incidentally is the greatest motivator in the world. After several hours of discussion, I advised him that I had to go to another appointment and wrapped up our discussion. Now here is the interesting point. I never made any comments or recommendations about his particular situation, but he shook my hand and looked right into my eyes and said, "Thanks for coming over, I feel so much better!" Now I want you to think about that. I didn't do anything, except listen to him talk and express his feelings. But he thinks

I made him feel better. Guess what? He made himself feel better! That is a classic example of why I say, "Happiness is a Choice!"

Think about people you know who either look happy all of the time or look sad all of the time. Next time you are around one of them, carefully watch and listen to them. See for yourself what they say or do, and what it is that gives you the impression that you have of them. Listen to their selection of words! Happy people use words like "can, will, sure, of course, etc." Sad people like words like "can't, won't, no, not, impossible, etc."

Some of the classic displays of unhappy people, actually make me laugh inside, now that I better understand them. For example, have you ever said to someone, "Good morning, how are you doing today?" And then they say to you, "Ok, I guess!" or "Not really good!", or "Terrible! Well, you can easily guess which type of person this is, not a very happy one. Here's a secret to happiness, regardless of what kind of day you are having or are faced with always say something positive. If I am having the worst day of my life, I will always say, "I am great today, how about you?" This will automatically cause several things to happen. First of all, *the person* who asked you this question, will be impressed with your upbeat response. Second of all, *you* will be impressed with this upbeat response. Now that's cool! The real experts in the world on practicing this are the Filipino people. They can be having the worst day of their lives, but you will never know it. This is one of the reasons why 11% of the Republic of the Philippines Gross Revenue annually is from foreign workers remittance! They know what I'm saying here.

Who You Associate With

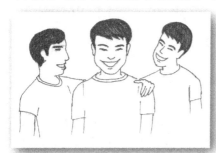

Sometime ago, I was really fascinated by a show I watched on Public Television, which was all about a study on happiness. It really zeroed in on the subject and there were some very interesting facts. They said that their study showed that happiness is very contagious and it spreads among people very fast. So if people come in contact with someone who is very happy it makes them happy and in turn makes others happy. I like that idea and I think I have experienced that often in my life. I know for sure it is a great feeling to be around someone who is happy and it's almost as good as being happy yourself. I bet you have had the same experiences if you really think about it.

Of course, I am also thoroughly convinced that the opposite is true. If your around someone who is terribly unhappy that is contagious too. So I solve that by avoiding unhappy people like the plague. Unhappy people also tend to hang out with other unhappy people. Negative people surround themselves with other negative people. It's like an alcoholic doesn't really want to be around sober people, because it doesn't feel good. But that same alcoholic loves to be around alcoholics, because it reinforces his or her behavior. So it is with unhappy people. Nothing is more disgusting to an unhappy person than to be around a really happy person. It's like saying, "I'm unhappy and I don't want anyone around who's going to ruin it for me". Sounds silly, huh? But that's the truth of the matter. Now if you sit around with them and talk about how unhappy you are, then it will be great for them. Years ago, I was working with a person who was unhappy and negative about everything and it was really starting to annoy me. So one day I said, "I can't imagine anything that would make you happy, can you? I believe if someone gave you a million dollars on a silver platter, you would be unhappy. You would probably complain that the platter was only silver and not gold." Wow! I was sorry I said that, because we didn't talk much after that. On the other hand, I didn't have to listen to all of that negativity every day, so it really turned out for the best. As my good friend Rick says, "I am allergic to negativity".

It has often been said and written, "We are a product of our environment", I know that is very, very true. So if you can agree with that, then you should also agree that you will become a product of who you hang out with. This subject of association, is one that always amazes me. I have met so many people who truly have a happy personality, but keep pushing it into the background by hanging out with the wrong people. Remember it's so simple, "if you hang out with negative people, you will be negative". Look up the statistics on what professions have the highest rate of suicide and you will find that Psychiatrists and Psychologists are at the top of that list. Vice versa, "if you hang out with positive people, you will be positive". So the choice is yours! Who do you really prefer to hang out with and what do you want to be, "negative" or "positive", "happy" or "sad"?

I have spent a great deal of my time studying success and what are the differences between people who succeed and those who don't. Later, when we talk about attitudes, self-esteem, and goal setting, I will go into this topic in more detail. But for now I want to share just a few simple things with you. Winners do not hangout with losers. They sympathize with them, and actually listen to them, particularly if they are people who are close to them in their lives. However, they never agree with them, nor offer support for their misconceptions or negative ideas.

I am a big fan of the great author Napoleon Hill, who wrote many great books, the first of which is "Think and Grow Rich". Mr. Hill is known as the master of defining the secrets of success. His subjects for his research are some of the greatest men in history. Henry Ford, Andrew Carnegie, J.P. Morgan, Thomas Edison, just to name a few, who incidentally were good friends with each other and Mr. Hill.

Napoleon Hill says that we all have the ability to share the knowledge of the universe, if we just open our minds to it. He also says that we must be the keepers of the door to our mind and be careful to only leave it open to positive and meaningful things and close it to negative and useless things. Now that's an interesting concept, isn't it? We are in charge of the door to our mind and we can decide what we let in and what we don't let in! So how do we do that? I think it's fairly simple. We can listen to negative things, but we don't have to open the door and let those thoughts get in there permanently to influence us. This is a process that requires a great deal of conditioning and practice. I found out that one way to do this is to constantly tell yourself that you are not going to take anything negative that you hear too seriously. I often listen to people telling me negative things and I respond by saying, "I see", "Ok!", "Oh!", or something like that. But then I forget that information faster than a group of Germans running to the bar when someone shouts "Free Beer". (With a name like Shankweiler, I can say that without any prejudice!)

Behavior

Mindset

IN LIFE YOU'RE either the steam roller or the pavement. Which one you are now, and which one you will be in the future, is determined by your mindset. Let me give you a quick lesson on mindset.

We all operate from two different mindsets. Negative or Positive! The key word associated with Positive Mindset is "confidence". The key words associated with Negative Mindset are "uncertainty" & "doubt". Which mindset dominates determines where you are in life and where you will go. Developing the correct mindset allows you to make decisions, in a routine way that are the right decisions that will strengthen your life.

I have always taught in my leadership classes that leaders are not born, but developed. Do you think you were born with confidence? The answer is "no"! Then how do we get it? Through development. Confidence can be grown just like a muscle. Do you think the world we live in is designed to reinforce the confidence in us? No! Studies on children from around the world indicate that the first three words a child typically learns are "mama", "papa", and "no". So imagine that if one of the first three words a child learns is negative, what are the chances for having a negative tendency?

What are some of the things we are being taught? To focus on problems rather than solutions, to complain about unfairness, inequality and hundreds of other real or imaginary injustices. Since we live in a day and age of rapid change (fueled by technology, which we will discuss later), and things keep changing at an ever increasing rate, what do you think this change brings to people who lack the confidence to adapt? It brings uncertainty and drives them into their "comfort zone". Our comfort zone is that place people try to hide out and avoid transformation. How comfortable do you think the comfort zone will remain? Sooner or later, it will becomes a very uncomfortable place to be!

I don't believe there's a person on the planet who should feel anxious, guilty, or unproductive on a regular basis. Every person should feel confident, powerful, and be proud of him-or herself, and should feel a sense of purpose. Unfortunately, I think most people discover, after a little introspection, that they aren't living in the Positive Mindset. They aren't living with confidence and their denying themselves the right to live with a greater sense of fulfillment and subsequently happiness.

Now how does this apply to you and what we're learning here? If you have doubt and can't overcome those feelings it doesn't matter how well the information, training, coaching you have available to you is, you won't be able to apply it. That's why you need to learn where your confidence resides and be able to draw upon it whenever you want.

Attitudes, "Yours and Others"

"Attitude" - The longer I live, the more I realize the impact of attitude on life. Attitude, to me, is more important than facts. It is more important than the past, than education, than money, than circumstances, than failures, than successes, that

what other people think or say or do. It is more important than appearance, giftedness or skill. It will make or break a company...a church...a home. The

remarkable thing is we have a choice every day regarding the attitude we will embrace for that day. We cannot change our past...we cannot change the fact that people will act in a certain way. We cannot change the inevitable. The only thing we can do is play on the one string we have, and that is our attitude...I am convinced that life is 10% what happens to me and 90% how I react to it. And so it is with you...we are in charge of our attitudes."

BY CHARLES SWINDOLL

"Attitude" – what an interesting and challenging word. Here are a few of the definitions offered in the Merriam-Webster Dictionary:

a: a mental position with regard to a fact or state <a helpful *attitude*>

b: a feeling or emotion toward a fact or state.
A simple definition that I like to use is "Attitudes are feelings and outlooks, which are internal to us. They are fairly stable, fixed, contrary to opinions that can change rapidly".

The definition seems at first quite simple, and in fact when we are looking at our own attitudes it's quite easy. But when it's someone else's attitude, it's not so easy to define or describe accurately. This word is so elusive and hard to define, that in my workshops on *Leadership* and *Supervision,* I always direct my students to place their focus on behavior and not on attitude. A person's behavior can be seen, heard, and described, while attitude can only be assumed. Attitude is internal to each individual and we can only guess what it is. When making decisions affecting others, it is dangerous to guess.

However, inside of ourselves, we see and feel our own attitudes. And more importantly, we have the power to determine our attitudes about ourselves and others. In other words, we are the sole determining factor of what our attitude is in a specific situation. It is important to keep in mind that our attitudes are greatly affected by our own perceptions and by whatever outside influences we decide to let in. So if we hang around with people who project negativity, hatred, dislike, worry and the whole array of beliefs that drive us down, we will impact our own attitude with theirs. And so it is visa-versa, if we hang out with those who are positive and happy, we are ourselves will be more likely to be positive and happy. This isn't rocket science, it is only common sense.

For some time now, I have been watching world events unfold such as economic, political, and social changes, many of them reported typically by the media as taking negative turns. Yet, in the midst of all of this reported turmoil, I find that I can either get immersed and absorbed by all the world events, including the political scene, stock markets, catastrophe's, wars, civil unrest, terrorism, etc., etc., or I can look at these things and yet remain mentally detached. Some days I begin to get immersed and when I recognize this happening, I immediately attempt to withdraw from that depth of involvement and I say to myself, "Hey, wait a minute, you can't do anything about this, so why should I worry?" What I have just told you is definitely *one of the main connections to the secret of being happy*, even in the middle of chaos. Somehow this doesn't seem like normal behavior, because we have always been taught to be so concerned, so worried, so immersed, about everything by the example of others around us, and yet that is not true.

There are choices here, once again, as the message of this book is trying to relay to you. We can chose to drown in worry, feel sorry for ourselves, and all that stuff, or say, "so what?" That doesn't mean that we don't care or aren't concerned! It means I can't do anything about it so I'm not going down the "depression, feel sorry about everything, or wish I would have" path. It is not necessary! I am going down the path of, "thank god I'm alive and well, eating something every day, got a roof over my head, enjoying a simple life and all the beautiful things and people around me". Isn't that worth something? Try it, you might like it better than the alternative.

When I think about the word "worry", I am always amazed at how much people worry about something, for absolutely no valid reason. I want to share with you a simple solution, which has been expressed by others over the years, about worrying. It's simple! Refuse to worry about anything that you do not have direct control over. If you can't control it, why worry about it! For me, I might care or be concerned about whatever it is, but I refuse to worry about it. Why should I, I can't change it! Am I concerned about war in the world? Absolutely! Am I concerned about terrorism in the world? Absolutely! But do I worry about these things? Absolutely not! I can't do anything about them, on a world scale. You should worry only about things that "you can do something about". Improving your life, your education, your earnings, your health, caring for your family, loved ones, friends, are some of the main things you should be focused on and that you can really have an impact on.

Here's a fun exercise for you to do, that I use in my Stress Awareness Workshop. I am not sure where this exercise came from, but it has been around for many years. Find a quiet undisturbed place to sit down. Get a pad and pencil and make a list of everything that you worry about. Put down family things, world events, work things, your local environment, friends, etc. Make the list as big as you can. Then make a chart like the one shown here and read carefully the description inside each space. Next assign each of your worry list items to one of the spaces and transfer that worry to that space.

Things I Worry About, That I Can Do Something About!	Things I Don't Worry About, That I Can Do Something About!
Things I Worry About, That I Can't Do Anything About!	Things I Don't Worry About, That I Can't Do Anything About!

When you are done, answer this question, "Which of these categories should I be worrying about?" The answer is simple and clear! *"Worry only about things you can do something about!" Forget the rest.*

If we think about it, whenever we encounter an individual, that we think doesn't have the right attitude, we usually see someone who gossips, meddles in others affairs, doesn't say nice things and more importantly worries about a vast array of things in the world. These people portray the "Woe is me!" syndrome. I refuse to be like that, and you should too.

I have met so many people in my life who clearly demonstrate they are happy, despite their socio/economic status in life. As a matter of fact, while thinking about writing this section, I came to realize that in my lifetime I have met more poor people who are happy than rich people who are happy. Many of my so called successful friends are those who ask me the most about what it takes to be happy. Now that's interesting, if you really think about it. For sure, it proves that money or success is not the secret to being happy. I always liked the quote, "money is the root of all evil". Of course, I have said a hundred times that I would like to have the whole tree. Ha! But money is one of the most prevalent reasons why many people feel unhappy. I hope you noticed that I didn't say the lack of money, but money is the reason. And this my friends, stems from attitude.

I would much rather be associated with a person who has little material value, but a great attitude about life and his/her surroundings, then be with a person who is a millionaire and just can't get along with anyone.

It has taken me many years to grasp the concept of enjoying the here and now. I must still remind myself every day, because I am one of those people who is always planning the future, thinking of new ideas, places, courses, lessons, etc., etc. But my life is just fine right now, right where it is right now. We can so easily fail to appreciate simple things, right in front of us at any given point in our lives. Our family, friends, neighborhood, city, and our country. Our home, the food we eat, the simple things we have and enjoy, our favorite TV show, music, great books, nice scenery, our favorite chair, laying on the sofa, listening to the sounds of our neighborhood, and much more. When I jog in the morning, I see something new that I may not have noticed the day before and that's very exciting. New faces, a different car, a tree that has an unusual shape, an animal, the way the wind is blowing and so on and so on. So make sure you look around yourself and enjoy the here and now. And always remember, your place in the universe is exactly where it is supposed to be at this moment. There is a plan and a reason for why you are here, doing whatever it is that you're doing. It is not an accident! Some of us are facing adversity and hardship, but it's part of the plan. Some are experiencing joy and success, its part of the plan. All of these things come to each and every one of us in their turn and when the universe decides they should or should not happen. So relax, and enjoy the ride! Be Happy!

Self-Esteem and Confidence

**If you think you can,
you probably will!
If you think you can't,
you probably won't!**

HENRY FORD

In this section I will give you the basics of "self-esteem and confidence" and then talk about how you can improve your self –esteem and confidence.

In recent years, I have had the opportunity to present the subject of "Self-Esteem and Confidence" in various countries and large venues. One such opportunity was in the Philippines. This work was part of an overall program intended to improve the "Interview Success Rate" of Filipino college graduates entering the Call Center Industry. It was one of those assignments where the result proved to be just as educational and interesting to me as it was to my students. I was real focused on the 'cultural differences" between the interviewer and the interviewee and how the projection of the candidate has such a dramatic impact on the outcome. In the Philippines people generally exhibit a "passive" behavioral style, as a result of their cultural and childhood experiences. In America, the behavioral style is generally "assertive", again as their cultural and childhood experiences dictated. If both parties in an interview situation do not have a fundamental understanding of these differences, one can clearly see how misperceptions, particularly about self-esteem and confidence, can develop and how a good candidate can be mistakenly rejected.

Incidentally, I am really fascinated at how many of the companies in the Call Center/Business Processing Outsourcing Industries still don't get this idea, nor teach their employees these behavioral/ cultural differences. I see these foreign companies, particularly in the Philippines, bringing in their home countries Human Resource people to teach the workers how to deal and cope with foreign clients and how to answer the clients, but in a manner that's like programing a robot. If the client says this, then respond with that, typical response training. Then is it a wonder they experience high turn-over rates, stress, alcohol/drug related illnesses and families asking what happened to my nice, passive son or daughter who never used the word "no" until they got this job.   I have tried to penetrate this market and give these young people a better understanding and explanation of how the client thinks versus how the Filipino thinks due to behavioral and cultural differences.   Wouldn't it be nice if these workers could come in and go to their locker and get their "Assertive Suit of Armor" on, do their job and then put the suit back in the locker on the way out and still retain their "passive" personality that mom and pop expect, and the world loves? In a later chapter I will write more about getting a "Suit of Armor".

Anyway while working to put my experience with these differences into a formal presentation, I came to realize that most of the people that I talked to, really didn't have a basic understanding of the true meaning of "self-esteem and confidence".   I really wanted to drive home several points about self-esteem and confidence in a way that would peak my students interest in this subject.

During the course of the development of this International Presentation, I realized just how strong our perceptions of self-esteem and confidence have been influenced by external sources. It also became very evident that our feelings about ourselves are universally affected by the huge media and commercial blitzes that we are subjected to day in and day out. The influence is enormous and leads us to pursue perfection, mainly through material things.

Confidence is power but it can be shattered in an instant. We can use athletes as a good example of how this occurs. Perhaps you have been watching your favorite show or sport and you have seen one of your idols fail to perform or make a mistake. Singing off key, stumbling in a beauty pageant, not scoring a goal at a critical time, striking out in baseball, fouling out of a basketball game, throwing an interception in American football, etc. In a matter of seconds that person goes from being extremely confident to becoming uncertain and ineffective. If he or she doesn't know how to get their confidence back they will fall into a slump, stop playing "to win" and then start playing "not to lose". So now, how will they play for the rest of the game? Ineffectively! But the really greats like LeBron James, Serena Williams, Manny Paquio, Phil Mickelson, Adelle, they know how to get back into their "confidence zone". How do you think they can do that? They developed a pattern of action thru focus on positive things. Are these stars or athletes the only ones who have to do this in order to excel? Of course not, all of us have to!

Remember we are only at our best when we are in a "Positive Mindset". What few of us ever discover is that there are some simple strategies to renew your confidence very quickly. I've seen people practice these techniques, again and again and again, to build confidence—and build it and build it. Then all of a sudden it becomes automatic for them, like it was for LeBron and Serena. I like to relate it to a reservoir or bucket that is attached somewhere inside our body. When something positive happens the confidence bucket fills up. When something negative happens the bucket wants to tip over and empty.

Can we get this confidence from a pill? No! Can technology bring this to us? No! Is it a choice we make to maintain a confident mindset and keep the bucket full or live with uncertainty and let the bucket dump out? Yes! Are we locked into one mindset or another? No! Does age, gender, nationality, background, ability, or social status have anything to with it? No!

Building a surplus of confidence is not difficult to do. I want to share with you surefire strategies you can use, starting today, to strengthen your self-confidence.

Strategy #1 - Feed your confidence daily

Consider this: If you went a whole day without eating, do you think you'd get hungry? Do you think your body would get weak? Yes and Yes! Your confidence needs nourishment too. You need to feed it daily for it to grow and get strong. What do you think we need to feed it? Success! Too many people wait for something big to happen in their lives before they reward themselves. When I talk about the differences between those who succeed with goals and those who don't, I mention that the successful people recognize their accomplishments every day and pat themselves on the back frequently. I want to teach you how to set up a game you can win every day. Here's how. Write down 5 specific things you have to have happen by the end of that day to feel successful. One or more may be simple things that are tied into your more extensive goals. I usually do it the night before. Remember they do not have to be complicated. It could be things like: workout for 20 minutes, complete your expense report, call someone, send an email, etc. Read this list in the morning and then review it before you go to sleep and consider each accomplishment a "win". Write a "W" next to those you actually did. So to get started get out your pen and write down 5 things that have to happen by tomorrow night for you to be able to look back to this moment and be pleased with what you've accomplished.

This exercise may sound trivial, it's anything but. It's an essential first step for keeping your "confidence reservoir" full.

Strategy #2 - Do feared things first

Look at your list and identify the item you have the most apprehension about. Ask yourself "which of the items on this list am I most likely not to accomplish, just because it's something that makes me uncomfortable?" Put a #1 next to that item. Why did we do this? If we don't the easy items get done and the more challenging objectives get put off. It's like back in high school. If they had multiple choice questions and essay questions, which ones did you do first? This assignment is completely opposite. Why? When you move towards your fear your confidence grows stronger. When you move away from your fear self-doubt takes the upper hand and confidence dies. Do this every day and you will soon see great results.

Strategy #3 - Honor Self-Promises

When you do #1 & #2 what are you really doing? Making a list of promises—to whom? Not to me, your friends, family, spouse, but to yourself. Who are we going to learn to trust via this process? Yourself! These guarantees, you make to yourself, although the easiest to break, are by far and away the most important ones to honor. You see, the very essence of confidence is self-trust. Would you trust anyone who lied to you repeatedly? People make promises to themselves that they don't keep all of the time. Can you think of some you have made recently and not kept? Can you erase those promises you made and didn't keep? Yes! Forget them and start anew!

It is easier for you to lie to other people than it is to lie to yourself. Self-perjury is and always will be a ferocious form of self-sabotage. What are the ramifications? You lose your sense of self, your confidence, your certainty, and you begin to imprison yourself. From this comes anxiety, guilt and it is the main reason why people don't use their potential. Remember the past doesn't equal the future. You can start to feel the powerful effects of this strategy by tomorrow at this time, if you just decide it's something you must do.

Strategy #4 - Focus on Progress, Not Perfection

Does perfection exist? No! You will need to forget the whole concept of perfection in order to strengthen your confidence. Perfection is an illusion. If you continue to pursue it, in your career, your relationships, your body, your life, all you will have to look forward to is a continual sense of deficiency, failure and uncertainty.

However, if you focus on progress or things you can actually measure you will have a growing sense of achievement and ever-strengthening level of confidence. This is why individuals who make achieving a dream their goal will be trying to achieve something that can't be achieved. For example, if my "goal" were to help everyone in America to become debt free, I would be so frustrated and so unhappy and so concerned about my failure that it would destroy me. And this would happen in spite of the fact that I helped thousands of people discover these strategies. What if I set a goal of 100,000 people in the next year? I could measure my progress and feel accomplishment.

How many people have we seen in the entertainment industry, who seemed to have everything, fame, fortune etc., but despite all the success, did not lead happy lives? Elvis Presley, Marilyn Monroe, Prince, Robin Williams, etc.. Why? Because they never had a good understanding of what we're learning here in this book. For many of these people it's because they were chasing dreams not goals.

Again, does perfection exist? Is there a perfect car, ring, house, phone, tv, etc., etc., etc. No! Can we however improve? Yes! Every situation you can mention can improve and we can improve constantly, by achieving and celebrating progress.

What can we conclude and develop from all of this? A feeling of certainty, a belief in our abilities, the confidence to move forward in spite of all the obstacles that stand in our way. We've all constructed this illusion of what perfection is. We've been taught that perfection is the ultimate success. We seek the perfect body, perfect mate, and perfect job. But these things don't exist. You must learn to see progress as success or every day is going to feel like a failure. It's a trap! So set up a game in which you can win. Set goals and use your daily list to let yourself succeed.

Where Should We Look? – Inside/Outside?

During the course of our search for answers to satisfy our need to understand ourselves, we often are confronted with choices and decisions, pertaining to where we should look. One of those choices that confronts us is whether we should look "in-

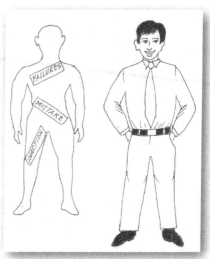

side" or "outside" of ourselves for answers. I want to share some things that I have developed, or things I have learned or heard from others pertaining to this subject. But right now I want you to know that my general consensus is that looking *inside produces more negative* feedback and looking *outside produces more positive* feedback. Of course, I don't expect everyone to agree with this, and that's ok too. So let me explain myself!

INSIDE

It is my strong belief that looking inside of ourselves, too often or too hard, for answers is typically a negative process and usually produces negative results. We tend to hide away so many bad things that happened in our lives and we want to label them as our failures, mistakes, inaction, etc., etc. No matter what the circumstances, we have labeled them and the labels are very hard to remove, like indelible ink or like the price sticker's stores put on merchandise, you know the ones we can never get off easily. And to make it worse, human nature is such that we want to get these things out of the dark corners of our memories, where they are full of cobwebs and dust and inaccuracies, and as they get older, major distortions of reality. Usually looking "inside" forces us to see some of these, because the labels are very big and stand out from all the other labels in our mind, and it typically clouds our ability to find something positive. Of course, this isn't a 100% guaranteed, but the likelihood of seeing something negative is far greater when we look inside ourselves that when we look outward and at others in the world.

We all know that our personal experiences greatly influence our perceptions, attitudes and behavior. So it just makes good sense, that what's inside of our minds is going to be heavily affected by these experiences and not necessarily reflective of the real world. If that's true, it's only sensible that the opposite is true when we look outside.

OUTSIDE

It's very hard to look outside of ourselves and not be able to see so much good. That's not to say that we never see anything bad, because we do and will always be confronted with that, unless we live like hermits and never go out. But when one considers all the sources available outside of ourselves, when searching for answers, it's so much vaster than the limited, biased history that's stored inside of us. The possibilities of seeing positive things is greatly enhanced by looking outside, that it's not even a fair contest to compare the two. When we look outside we have unlimited resources to tap into, vast amounts of knowledge, experience, examples, viewpoints, etc. The majority of this information is virtually all positive and this is why I believe that we need to look outside of ourselves for good positive answers. Of course, we must also gain some agreement with our inner selves to be comfortable with the answers we finally conclude, but I think you can get the picture of what I'm saying.

Basically, what I'm saying is this. When I am searching for answers to personal decisions or wanting to find my true feelings about things, I would much rather prefer to look outside of myself, rather than inside. When I look inside, I have a tendency to come up with a lot of negative baggage and it clouds my ability to see a true and positive picture. This doesn't mean that I'm a bad person, but I'm human and human nature works this way, whether we like it or not. You will have to ponder this choice for yourself and decide what you want to do. But I assure you there is so much more to see that is positive by looking outward and moving forward than there is to looking inward and trying to move backward. Try it, you might like it!

CHAPTER 3

Life Conditions

Change

THIS IS ONE of the most interesting topics I have ever encountered, particularly in the time period we are now living in. I cannot remember any time in my life, in which so much change is occurring, so rapidly and in so many different ways. As all of us have done, I observed change in so many ways in my lifetime, some for the good, some not so good, but always change has been there, lurking around the corner, waiting to challenge us. It has been said many times and has been confirmed that "change is usually very uncomfortable". I know in many of my seminars I have taught people that being "too comfortable" with ourselves is not always good, because if we are too comfortable it can mean we are not growing and that's not good. So if that's true, then what is the answer to the question, "how comfortable should we be"? Well, I can tell you right now, there is no fixed answer that suits all! Some of us want to be constantly challenged, never standing still, in constant motion, always changing. Others, want some challenge, like to stand still once in a while, changing sometimes. And still some, wanting no challenges, standing still always, never wanting to change. The later have a serious problem, which I think we can all appreciate, but I don't find any pleasure, nor any point, in going into more detail about that lifestyle and therefore I will let you draw your own conclusions about them. It is my hope however, that I can in some small way, show them a path in life that is a great deal happier and more rewarding, and hence one of the reasons for this book.

With that said, let me move on. I believe the majority of us fit into the first two categories, 'constant change, challenge', or 'some of both'. And that's great, as we will continue to grow and learn and hopefully enjoy our lives, careers, etc. I want to emphasize here that it is not my intent to tell you, or attempt to identify change in your life or really how much is best for you, because we both know that's impossible to do. I do want to talk about how the world has changed and engage you on the subject of living in a "Dynamic State", meaning constantly in motion, turning, rotating, never stopping, or in a "Static State", meaning standing still, no motion, stopped, etc.

As human beings, I think we are designed to only be able to take so much of either of these two states. There must be some sort of balance level for you and one for me and for all others in this world. I don't know what that is! But what I want to do is address what's going on in the world right now, relative to these two states of human condition and challenge. And to do that, I can only offer you my personal opinions and observations as I see and feel these "Dynamic & Static States" in my surroundings. I believe that we are experiencing too much of a "Dynamic State" in the present world and that we as human beings, are not afforded enough of the "Static State" in which to settle down and stabilize.

Being an engineer as well as a psychologist, I appreciate that us human beings operate as fine-tuned piec-
es of machinery, with many sophisticated systems, all
operated by a master computer, which has an operating system and a computer program, governing
it. I recall years ago, when after much encouragement from a colleague, I visited an Acupuncturist
for a problem I was having with headaches and neck
pain. Now this experience was a rather humorous
one to begin with, as I was very reluctant to seek alternative solutions and had some very preconceived
notions about them. The first notion I had in my
brain, was that an acupuncturist had to be an Asian
with a name like Wen Lei and must come from a far
off place like China or India. Secondly, this person
had to be a third, fourth or fifth generation Guru,
having had centuries of this knowledge engrained
in his/her brain through hereditary genetics, and
family lineage. This was immediately dismissed
when my friend set up an appointment for me with
his doctor, and on my first visit I was shocked to discover that he was a red-headed Jewish guy, whose
hobby was playing in a Jazz Band as a percussionist.
Man, was I surprised, and to top it off, he was one
the coolest guys I have ever met. The last I heard, he
is still located in Dartmouth, Massachusetts and has
a very successful Acupuncture Practice.

So here I was in the acupuncturists office having a discussion with him about my condition and he summed things up very simply, treated me, and with a few more visits I was relieved of the headaches and neck pain. During this time, several engineering terms were used to explain to me what he thought was going on with my body system and what was causing these problems. I am going to take the liberty here to borrow and share his analogy with you, in order to further expand upon the theory of "too much Dynamic State".

As some of you already guessed or concluded, the problem I was having was directly attributed to "Stress and Tension". Our brains, and the respondent systems, respond to our computer program. Like so many programs in the world, they start out as simple programs with basic logic blocks, saying if this happens do that, and if that happens do this, etc. They look like a simple flowchart, with a series of connected blocks moving down a page and arrows connecting the blocks. But then after some time, a new programmer comes on board and starts to add blocks and lines, and the whole thing gets a little more complicated, until after a long period of time, the program becomes a monster and when the programmer leaves, no one is sure how it works. So it is with our brains' computer, but the additions are made to accommodate life's stresses and strains, and after a while we don't even know why we are experiencing things that are happening. So the solution is to take the system down, and reprogram it to a simple level and start all over. Of course, all the basic parts have to remain intact so we continue to live and function as regular human beings. Just bypass all the crazy unexplained blocks of code, getting back to something understandable. Basically, this is what happens in the human nervous system when Psychologist's years ago used electroshock treatments on mental patients. It's like our own laptop or desktop, once in a while it locks up, and we shut it down, and then everything seems to straighten out. Not a very scientific explanation, but one I could understand. So my treatment was several sessions of acupuncture to relieve the tension in my muscles and system and sure enough it worked. Back to the basics!

So here is my contention! When we are constantly forced to operate in a Dynamic State, we build up huge amounts of stress and since there is very little time in the Static State, we never get back to our basic program. Look around you! If you're like the rest of us, everything in the world is constantly changing now, and if you don't seek some refuge, you are in the never ending Dynamic State. So my contention is that we are bombarded with too much change and is taking its toll on us.

So what to do? Easy, we have to create our own Static State and put ourselves into it regularly. Time away from multi-tasking, work, computers, internet, news, etc., all the things that keep us stressed. We must find a place that puts us into the Static State. For me, it is on the golf course. I don't go there to really play golf, because nothing I do there can be construed as golf anyway. Always in the woods, water, or where I'm not supposed to be, like the other fairway. But most importantly I'm not online, in my office, planning, reading, hearing bad news, thinking about money, etc., etc. I'm just out there on the golf course with the grass, trees, birds, worms and usually with some crazy and fun friends. The world literally stops!

Remember, we are all so different and we manage to find our own ways to reprogram ourselves. Believe or not, I can put myself into the Static State, by being on a stage in front of an audience at a seminar or at a public event. For me this is heaven, teaching someone, learning from them, watching and listening to their responses, accomplishing something good. No stress for me there, but absolute pleasure. It's like I said earlier about one of the real secrets of happiness, "Find Something You Love to do, And Then Get Someone to Pay You to do it'!

So think about all of this and add your own ideas and thoughts to this. Look around you and see what's Dynamic and what's Static! Determine how much of each you need or want and formulate your own plan to manage these two states. After all its "Your Life" isn't it?

A really interesting concept that has been coming to the surface in the past several years, is that of downsizing one's own life. Well, I learned that when I went bankrupt and got a divorce. I left the US Mainland, went to the Philippines on business, at first, and then hung out there until I was basically completely broke. I moved to Saipan and stayed with my son. My son and his family were so very good to me but because of my circumstances I was pretty miserable for quite some time. Talk about a major down-sizing! I eventually found a small room, with a crude bathroom, and no kitchen. This was in a house, downstairs next to the garage in a friend of my daughter-in-law's house. The landlord helped me make a simple outside kitchen on the small concrete porch outside the entrance door. I put a small plastic sink with a hose attached to it, a small wooden table next to it and then bought a portable single burner gas stove to cook on. My room had a bed, a small TV, my clothes and a small office type refrigerator. These were truly the basics and I never would have imagined I could learn to live with so little, but I did. Of course, on Saipan, I came to realize that there were thousands of people who lived like that, mainly the overseas foreign workers, who worked in the hotels and garment factories.

After many months and rebounding, I eventually wound up renting the whole house with a nice sized living room, dining room, kitchen, two bedrooms and a bath and converting my former downstairs small room into an office space. But I never forget that I was perfectly happy in my single room and it was where I lived when I met my wife and we spent many hours sitting on the bed and watching that small TV, with just a small fan to cool us, in the tropical climate.

People who meet me today, might think that I have always lived in a great successful world and have never had any problems. Ha! For the majority of the time that I spent writing this book, I was in my 60's, living on a small pension and social security, occasionally getting a speaking engagement, or small consulting job and that's it. My life was simple, living on a small island that was economically depressed and lacking in leadership. Couldn't drink the water out of the faucet, because it's like sea water, cable tv that's not even up to third world standards and expensive power rates that are some of the highest in the U.S. The internet service is rated the 2nd slowest out of 160 places and countries tested. Thousands of foreign workers, many who have been there for 10, 15, 20, 30 years, and are still treated as temporary with no chance of U.S. status, and are left in limbo by immigration regulations that don't come close to the reality of current economic and development needs, human rights, and plain old common sense. Basically this all stems from some who are happy to use them and then discard them and a bureaucratic Congress, governing the US Immigration System that follows the political climate more than actual needs.

Yet, I refused to let those things govern my life. Instead, I have hundreds of those foreign workers as my friends, laugh my butt off when the politicians do crazy things, chuckle at the TV Cable service, and continue to frustrate the hell out of others by being so damned happy. It's wonderful and it doesn't get any better than that. The island is so beautiful, that all I have to do is stop, whenever I feel myself slipping into the proverbial mold, and just look around at all the beauty surrounding me.

Do I ever get depressed? Of course I do! But I am not depressed or unhappy for very long, because I refuse to make that choice. And you have the same option, if you just learn how to exercise it. Oh, you will have lots of people tell you that's not possible or normal, but look at who's telling you and how they live their lives. Human nature is such that everyone likes to tell us a million reasons why we <u>can't</u> do something, and hardly any reasons why we <u>can</u>. If you would like to prove this to yourself, just select a simple question to ask a bunch of people to test this theory. Make something up, if you have to! Like ask, "Do you think I would do well as a business person (or cook, consultant, teacher, mentor, business owner, etc.)? Don't even think about the question, but concentrate on the diversity of the answers you will get and how much sense they make. If you ask five people you will get five different answers. Ask fifty people, fifty different answers. Unless of course the answer must be one word like, yes or no, good or bad, etc. I have this philosophy that I enjoy hearing my friend's opinions, but I only care about what I feel inside and nothing else. When we look at the history of so many successful and accomplished people, we find that most people around them believed whatever they were doing wouldn't work. Thomas Edison's family tried to have him committed to a mental institute, because he kept talking about a machine you could talk into and it would playback your voice. Bill Gates told his friends at Harvard that he will make it possible for the average person to operate and have a computer. What a goofball idea that was at the time?

You see, you have to set your own course, as much as possible. You have to decide that no matter what that course is, whether you determine it or life dictates it, many times in the form of change, you are going to choose to be happy for the majority of that trip. Being happy is the greatest reward that life can offer, more than wealth or anything else. I have had so many ups and downs in life that I couldn't even begin to describe them, but the bottom line of all of that, is that I have been so happy for the majority of my life and I am so very grateful for that. So here you learned that change is a big part of that process. Change is good and you should embrace it. Remember that change is a part of "Happiness", the real gold at the end of the rainbow!

Dealing with Setbacks

No matter what we do or how well we plan, life will always deal us some setbacks. They are inevitable and are a normal part of life. Of course it's very important to note that at different stages in our lives, we tend to handle these setbacks in different ways. When  we're young, we basically just blow by them and keep doing whatever we're doing and most minor setbacks have very little impact. However, as we get older, the simplest setbacks can cause us a great deal of anxiety and discomfort.

I have been very interested in studying this subject, since as a senior citizen I am experiencing the very topic that I have been observing for all these years. It gives me an insight to attempt to constructively evaluate why I handle setbacks differently now than when I was younger. Why am I interested? Mainly, because if I can identify the differences in thinking, it becomes much easier to teach others how to better deal and handle life's setbacks, at whatever stage in life we are in. Younger people need to learn to take some of the setbacks more seriously and learn from them. Older people need to learn how to blow by them. Isn't this funny? Role reversal.

One thing in life that I have learned about this subject, is that whatever happens today, no matter how it appears, it will be different in our minds tomorrow. Many times, I have mistakenly identified events as setbacks, when in fact they were part of the normal progression of the event I was experiencing. For example some time ago, I created a temporary setback in my own mind while I was online checking to see if my Philippine Permanent Resident Visa had been approved. Having been involved with visa applications and processes for several years, I had begun to assume that something could and would probably go wrong. So when I received a notice telling me to check online to see if my visa had been approved, I couldn't find the folder for August on the immigration website. So I started to look at the last week of July and searched through a hundred or more names and found nothing. Then I did the same for the prior week, but nothing. Now my brain is saying something is wrong. Finally I asked my wife to call immigration and talk to someone. Lo & Behold my approval was listed under the July

16th folder and my certificate and card were waiting there for my pickup. For several days, I put myself through a whole series of "what if's" for absolutely nothing.

My wife received the following on Facebook as I was writing this and I couldn't believe at how appropriate the timing was, so I am sharing it with you.

A psychologist walked around a room while teaching stress management to an audience. As she raised a glass of water, everyone expected they'd be asked the "half empty or half full" question. Instead, with a smile on her face, she inquired: "How heavy is this glass of water?" Answers called out ranged from 8 oz. to 20 oz.

She replied, "The absolute weight doesn't matter. It depends on how long I hold it. If I hold it for a minute, it's not a problem. If I hold it for an hour, I'll have an ache in my arm. If I hold it for a day, my arm will feel numb and paralyzed. In each case, the weight of the glass doesn't change, but the longer I hold it, the heavier it becomes."

She continued, "The stresses and worries in life are like that glass of water. Think about them for a while and nothing happens. Think about them a bit longer and they begin to hurt. And if you think about them all day long, you will feel paralyzed – incapable of doing anything."

Remember to put the glass down.

("Thanks to Jim Harmon")

I don't know if Mr. Harmon is the author or if he simply posted this, so no offence to the author or Psychologist! Several good points are to be made from this. One is that as the Psychologist suggests we should not carry around unneeded, unnecessary baggage, which does nothing but weigh us down and wears us out. This point is self-explanatory and I don't think I need to expand on it further. The second is how we can control the management of supposed or perceived setbacks in reference to actual setbacks. The best advice I can give you is to take the time to digest a perceived setback and stand back for some period of time to see if that perception changes. I try very hard now to take a day or so to let the particular situation settle in and see how I see it after this period of time. Most generally things always look at their worst when we first see them or hear them. So step back and mentally play a game that sounds like this. "I'm not really sure what the facts are here, but I'm going to look and listen some more." This time lapse allows all the anxieties and misconceptions to fade somewhat and lets us see the real facts. I guess this fits the description of the old adage, "don't jump to conclusions!"

As far as real world setbacks, we should take the approach that they are going to happen, but the impact on us is entirely up to us. I find that sometimes if I simply laugh at something that comes along, it doesn't seem to hurt me as much. I'll use the example of a recent injury I experienced. Some time ago I developed serious pain in my left upper arm and shoulder. I couldn't identify any particular event relating to this pain and it was quite frustrating. I had played golf several days before, but no significant event had occurred there and I simply was mystified. I waited over a month before taking my wife's advice and visiting a doctor. After an x-ray and ultrasound, the doctor advised me that I have a torn tendon and discussions about the possible permanent loss of the use of my arm, if I'm not careful. Further testing, surgery, and physical therapy, were also discussed. My understanding from this session was that this was a grave situation with a potentially very negative outcome. I immediately imagined that I could never play golf again and I would now have a disability in addition to incurring significant medical expenses. I allowed myself to slip into a somewhat depressed state and after leaving the doctor's office I told my wife I needed a beer and needed to sit down and think. Although my wife kept telling me not to look at the worst side of this and be positive, I had a hard time getting a handle on all of my feelings and gathering my thoughts in an intelligent manner.

A few days later, my wife was talking to our neighbor, who is one of the head nurses at a well-respected hospital in the Philippines, and she requested the test results so she could share them with an orthopedic surgeon at her hospital for a second opinion. We accepted the invitation and in a few days I found myself sitting in the office of this surgeon and being examined again. This time the doctor advised that the situation might not be as serious and recommended that we take a single step approach to solving the problem. So the doctor suggested that we first attempt physical therapy at a clinic he highly recommended and see how that works out. After several weeks of physical therapy, which was very interesting and healthy for me, I improved dramatically and shortly thereafter started playing golf again. Yippee!

The point to be made here is that we must continue to look ahead at all of our options and move forward in a positive manner. I don't know what would have happened if my wife had not taken charge and mentioned this to my wonderful neighbor, who intervened and was smart enough not to accept one opinion. You see, I should have been looking ahead and instead of thinking of the doom and gloom, which clouded my good judgement. If in fact, I could not play golf anymore it's not the end of the world, it would simply mean I would have to spend more time at the sports bar drinking beer and watching golf. A positive outcome either way. Ha!

How Happiness is Affected by Predictability

In many cultures, predictability is the norm and is expected for us to lead a somewhat normal, sensible life. However, in some cultures, predictability is not expected and in fact unpredictability is the norm. I have found this to be a fascinating subject and one which can determine just how happy a person can be within certain surroundings. In America we expect a fair amount of predictability in our everyday lives. We are willing to expect a few unpredictable circumstances once in a while, but we really don't like too many surprises. So when something unpredictable happens we tend to over react and let it upset our balance and in most cases our feeling of being happy. A classic example of this is when we have a problem with something like our computer and we call a telephone number to get assistance and get a call center person. If the person doesn't respond the way we think they should we immediately feel insecure about the situation. For example if they were to ask us a simple question like, "Did you turn the computer on?" we could go ballistic. Ha! For many foreigners who are manning the call center lines, "unpredictability" is a normal part of their daily lives. I've lived in the Philippines, where unpredictability is the norm. There you never know what will happen on a day to day business with things like traffic, appointments, systems, services, etc. Every time I go to the market something unpredictable happens. Prices are not marked on items, the card swiping machine at my cash register isn't working, or a multitude of silly things happen. I have now learned that this is the norm and I expect it. So you could say I turned the unpredictable into the predictable. Wow! I'm impressed with that ability! But the reality is that I don't let these things ruin my happiness on a regular basis. Do I ever get upset at this unpredictability? Absolutely! However, not as much as I used to because if we want to remain happy, we need to adjust to our environments. Where I lived "poor service" was the norm. Imagine that! Here I was in the country that trains and sends hundreds of thousands of people around the world to work in the service industry, but in their own homeland they have the worst service on the planet. But the secret to dealing with that is simply facing this reality and so if that's what I expect I am not too upset when it comes. Now a real upside of this is that when good service comes into my life there, I am elated and over joyed! It's all in how we look at our circumstance and how we condition ourselves to deal with the unpredictable.

Of course, I would have loved to live in a more predictable world, but that's not where I had chosen to live. I compromised that side of myself for the benefits of the other things that came with living in the Philippines, such as really nice people, great weather, low cost of living, etc. Many of my ex-pat friends are miserable with this condition, mainly because they haven't stopped to look at what it really is. I hope they read this book! When asked about living in the Philippines I always respond by pointing out the good things I mentioned above and then pointing out that if you don't like unpredictability, don't go there!

For all of us, there will always be a side of life that is unpredictable. We get ill, people die, our jobs change, friends come and go, and in today's world we live in a constant state of flux. The technology that surrounds us makes tomorrow so unpredictable and also gives us pictures that change from day to day. One day Viber is the in thing, the next day it's What'sApp! Who knows what's coming tomorrow? For many generations, particularly mine, we always wanted to know what's coming and we want to be in charge when it comes. That era is gone and now we are simply servants to whatever comes tomorrow, whether we like it or not. But that's not so bad when we consider that the choices with what's out there is beyond our wildest imagination. Never would I have expected to have so many tools, services, games, etc. at my fingertips. So again it's taking charge of how we deal with unpredictability that has so much influence on our happiness. Every day that I wake up on the green side of the grass I am grateful and welcome everything that comes my way, whether it was predictable or not. With that in mind, it's pretty hard to get too bummed out at whatever happens. Usually, I like to think of those unpredictable things as fun challenges to which I have to use my intellect to deal with and work through. It beats the hell out of sitting around staring at the walls!

CHAPTER 4

Tools and Tips

The Right Way to Start Your Day!

I HAVE ALWAYS believed that the way you start your day, sets the tone for how things will go throughout the day. And so many people start their day in the wrong way that it makes it very difficult to recover for the rest of the day. I was guilty of this for most of my life, but now that I know how this all works, I make a genuine effort every morning to start out right. It has made a major difference for me and has made my life a lot more enjoyable. Let's look at the wrong way first and then we'll discuss what I perceive to be the right way to start each day.

There is nothing worse than waking up and thinking about something negative in the first few minutes. And nothing can do that for you better, than turning on the TV to the morning news. Who was shot, how many died, what a terrible car wreck, airplane crashes, celebrities getting divorced, and on and on and on. Now what do you think that will do for your attitude that day. What a horribly negative way to start your day. Don't do it? Keep that TV off, until you have had a chance to start the right way. Same with the radio and social media, which also like to tell us about all the negative things that happened yesterday or overnight. Your brain doesn't need that kind of food early in the day, so stop doing that to yourself. Later in the morning, or even on the way to work or school is ok to start getting tuned into what is going on in the world, but not when you first wake up. Also, don't' engage in any negative discussion with family members or others until you have had a chance to program your brain the right way. Those discussions can wait a few minutes, until you are awake and in a good mood, with your brain programmed to look at them in a more positive light.

Remember we become the product of what we hear and see and if what you hear and see the first thing every day is so negative, you will have a very good chance of starting out with some strong negative feelings, before you even have a chance to get started. It's like starting your car and then immediately holding the accelerator to the floorboard. Oil hasn't had time to circulate, other components are not warmed up, and the likelihood of blowing up the engine is pretty strong. I guarantee your engine won't like that treatment, any more than your attitude will like being treated like that.

What should you do when you wake up? Well, assuming that you've had a good night's sleep, which is so important to your well-being, you should have prepared yourself to go through a routine to feed your brain some really good positive and happy things. Let me illustrate my routine and then of course you can develop your own. When I wake up, I deliberately tune out all other thoughts that enter my mind, except of course going to the bathroom. I replace them immediately with thoughts of 'how lucky I am to be alive, in decent health, with a nice wife, good family and friends, able to eat, live in a decent house with a good roof over my head' and as many other things I can think of in this brief moment in time. Doesn't have to last long, just a few minutes to give you that warm, grateful feeling, before everyone else tries to screw it up. Ha! And as you know, there are plenty of people who like to mess up our good feeling, especially if they don't know how to feel that way themselves.

By the way, I also recommend this technique at bedtime. Think about how lucky you are to have a roof over your head, a nice warm bed, a companion, or whatever it is that you are blessed with. And no matter how poor or disadvantaged we are, we all can find something to be grateful for at the beginning and end of each day.

So now when you have all that good feeling running around inside of you, go ahead and tune into the world, but take it all in stride and use the ideas and suggestions I give you in this book about not worrying about things you can't change. The majority of news, things we hear from others, etc., is about things we can't do anything about. So why worry about them?

Dreaming

I have always been a dream-er, ever since I can remember. Winning the lotto, falling into riches, inventing things, building my own company, travelling around the world, or whatever else pops into my mind, I will dream about it. It's important here to distinguish between the two  types of dreaming that most people experience. We all are familiar with the night time or sleep dreaming we experience. But we also can find ourselves dreaming while wide awake, generally referred to as "Day Dreaming" and one of my favorite things to do. I also highly recommend that you should spend some time day dreaming, as it is fun, healthy, a good stress reliever, and many times incredibly constructive. In this section I will be focused on day dreaming and sharing with you some thoughts on the topic.

I am a true believer in the concept that we are what we think we are. If we don't have any great aspi-rations or dreams, we generally are pretty bland and generally don't have a very exciting or happy life-style. On the other hand, if we dream big, we have a much better chance of accomplishing those dreams, sometimes in an almost automatic way, without even thinking about it.

First of all, with dreams we have hope! Hope is a powerful motivator and stimulator. It is also the prime ingredient in believing. We've often heard that success is much easier achieved with a strong belief in ourselves and in what we are doing. No one really succeeds without believing and without hope. But plenty fail due to a lack of these two important life ingredients.

Secondly, with dreams we can visualize and see rewards. Every great inspirational, motivational, leadership and personal speaker or coach in the world will emphasize the importance and need to visualize our successes and accomplishments before they happen. See them happening, right in front of you. Well, there you go! Day dreaming is exactly that!

Thirdly, with dreams we are more likely to maintain a positive and healthy attitude in all we do each and every day. So what, if all our dreams never come true or don't happen? Just the dream itself is incredibly rewarding and most of all fun. We completely forget that life is supposed to be fun! We get so immersed in our day to day activities and responsibilities that we fail to recognize that we're only here for a certain period of time, unknown to us, and it's up to us how we spend that time.

At this juncture in my life, my biggest dream is tied directly to this book and one of my greatest ambitions. My dream is that when this book is completed and published, I will have a show highlighting the book and speaking to thousands of people about it. I can visualize the billboard on Roxas Blvd in Manila at the Philippine International Cultural Center (PICC) reading, "Spend an evening with Dr. Ken and learn why Happiness is a Choice". I can see it now as clear as day! The show will have some of my good friends as guests and hosts. I will use Bobby McFerrin's song "Don't Worry, Be Happy!" as the theme song, with his permission of course. Wow! The thought is so very motivating.

I prefer to be happy and when I am day dreaming I am one happy dude! Try it you might like it.

Be careful with sharing all of this with everyone, as the world is full of people who love to shoot holes in our dreams and overall happiness. Unhappy people can't stand happy people, because they are immersed in their own self-pity, etc., and we tend to interfere with that. Of course, there is also the jealousy factor, the "if I can't have it, why should you?" As I mentioned earlier, don't hang around with these type persons as they cannot be of any benefit to your success or well-being.

Once in a While Turn Everything Upside Down

Sometimes in life we find ourselves just continuously going with the flow with not much thought of doing things differently. We do this for months and months, years and years, and only occasionally think of other options as something way out there and not in our realm. The time passes by so quickly and we hardly notice it, and more importantly we fail to assess our options to change our lives. We get into our routines and in many ways its get way too comfortable. As I told you before, if we're too comfortable we're not growing or moving forward and more than likely not generating the happiness we really want or should be experiencing.

My wife and I moving to the Philippines, from the island of Saipan, is a good example of finally recognizing a need for change.   We kept talking about a move for years, but always found a reason not to do it. Finally in January of 2013, we decided we're going to move. My wife was working at the Hyatt Hotel in Saipan and saving most of her earnings, so we knew that by October 2013 we would have a small nest egg to lean on. Not much, but enough to cover our moving expenses and a few bucks left over. My retirement income would suffice for us in the Philippines and even leave a little extra each month. So after selling most of our household items and our car, we hopped on a plane for Manila on October 14th and set out on a complete new venture.

My wife's best friend in Saipan, Tet, helped us arrange to rent her sister's home in San Pedro, Laguna.

A lovely house and the owner was very happy to give us a very affordable monthly rent, because she has the house as an investment and the maid, who has been in her family for 46 years, was wanting to retire and go back to the province. So we were an ideal solution to her problem. Someone who was willing to allow her to keep many of her personal things in the house and also someone she could trust to take care of the expensive furnishings in the house.

So here we were, living a good life, making many trips to the malls and around the country and had even made a trip to Singapore, which was a fabulous experience. My brother-in-law is a manager in the casino at the Marina Bay Sands Hotel in Singapore, which is one of the most spectacular hotels in the world. Bottom line is that we should have done this earlier, but fear and apprehension kept us where we were. We got too comfortable with our setting, but yet all the time realizing we needed more sensory challenges, excitement, and a new setting away from typical island life. Incidentally, we have recently moved back to Saipan as we really missed this beautiful island life and our family and friends who are here.

I have always observed that when people are confronted with a major change in their life, they always adapt. Actually, earlier in my life I can remember moving because of my job and everyone in the family hating to have to move, but in six months when I wanted to return to our old location to visit family, no one wanted to go! So my suggestion to you is that if you are thinking about a change, keep all of what I just said in mind, because in months you will probably say you were glad you did.

Suit of Armor

One can't be happy 24/7, because we are human and life presents us with many challenges every day, some good, some bad. The good things kind of take care of themselves and we don't mind having too many of them, do we? But what do we do with the bad things that come along.

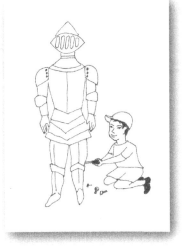

Well, first of all, they are inevitable and there will always be bad things that come our way. The real issue is how do we let them affect us? For many people small things can be devastating and for others they don't seem to really care or are not impacted in any significant way, by these minor issues. So why is that? Upon examination of these differences, we can easily see that some of us have a built in "suit of armor", that defends us from minor upsets. So if you are a person who easily gets upset by minor things that come your way, you have got to go out and obtain your own "suit of armor". Wow! Where do we buy that? At Walmart, Kmart, from a Psychiatrist or Psychologist, a TV show, or where?

Here's a surprise! We can't buy it and it's not on the market! So no matter how much we search for it, how much money we spend trying to find it, or how much suffering and misery we contribute to looking for it, it's not out there. Here's the secret to acquiring your own "suit of armor". You must develop it! And how do we do that? Just like every other characteristic of our personality was developed by us, as previously mentioned in this book, we must develop this part of our attitude in order to be able to fend off those feelings that want to come over us and make them bounce off of us and not disrupt our feelings of wellbeing and confidence.

Developing this "suit of armor" attitude is simple as long as we remember the lessons learned about how we decide how we want to feel or act. Only you can make the decision to be impacted by small things or to totally reject them and walk away. It begins by becoming conscious of a minor thing that happens that could disrupt your feelings, disregarding it, and then looking back and seeing how much better that process was then the alternative. Envision being able to say to yourself, "Wow! That just happened and I didn't react and it feels so much better". If you really think back to any of these minor events and how you reacted, you will clearly see that any grief you suffered was self-inflicted and could have been totally avoided. Like the book title says, "Happiness is a Choice", sub-titled "So Why Not Make it?"

The Value of Laughter

There has been a great deal written about the therapeutic value of laughter. Talk about an important part of living good! I don't think anything can replace what a good laugh can do for us. I know that when I laugh, I feel good for a long period of time afterward. A good laugh can change my entire day. If I start getting stressed, I will sit still and just think about something that really made me laugh hard. It might be something from yesterday or 20 years ago, who cares. But that same laugh can bring the same feeling to me over and over again. What a treasure. This is one of the reasons I love the internet so much. You can laugh everyday by going there, whether it's a joke from a friend or just something you run across while surfing and working on the net. Thanks Bill Gates, Steve Jobs, Thomas Edison, Mark Zuckerberg, Al Gore?, and more.

I particularly love YouTube because you can look up your favorite shows, comedians, etc. and view them again and again. It's so powerful due to the fact that the latest people, shows, etc. are there as well as all the old great classics. This is one of the great repositories of laughter in the world. I would highly recommend that you visit it regularly and make yourself LOL.

Being silly once in a while is also very important. I have special friends who allow me and themselves to just be silly. This is something that most adults think is only for children. Well, that might be true, but think about this. We all have the child that lived in us earlier, still living inside of us. So my theory is I want to let that child out occasionally and in the proper setting. It's really fun, try it!

CHAPTER 5

Observations

Correlation Between Love and Happiness

THESE ARE THE two most connected words in human language, in my opinion. If you love someone, something, or yourself, or any combination thereof, your happiness will definitely be influenced in a major way. As we know, this influence can be negative or positive depending upon the circumstances of the love relationship.

Love is such a powerful word and for all of history man has tried to clearly define and project all that is associated with this word. We all know there is no single simple definition that can properly justify or even begin to describe the true power of the word. More than any other word in human language, this word has attached to it the dynamics of feelings, emotions, and experience, which sometimes go beyond description. For the sake of offering an intellectual definition, Merriam-Webster Dictionary says –

Love *noun - Definition*
: a feeling of strong or constant affection for a person
: attraction that includes sexual desire : the strong affection felt by people who have a romantic relationship
: a person you love in a romantic way
Full Definition
: strong affection for another arising out of kinship or personal ties <maternal *love* for a)
: attraction based on sexual desire : affection and tenderness felt by lovers
: affection based on admiration, benevolence, or common interests <love for his old schoolmates>
: an assurance of affection, enthusiasm, or devotion <give her my love>
: warm attachment, enthusiasm or devotion <love of the sea>

: the object of attachment, devotion, or admiration <baseball was his first love>
: a beloved person : darling – often used as a term of endearment
:*British* – used as an informal term of address
: unselfish loyal and benevolent concern for the good of another: as **(1)** : the fatherly concern of God
5 : a god or personification of love
6 : an amorous episode : love affair
7 : the sexual embrace : copulation
8 : a score of zero (as in tennis)

Anyway, my point here is to show the direct connection between love and happiness. Nearly all of what is said here boils down to just plain common sense.

If we are in love and that love is of a positive nature, we are very, very happy. Being in love projects such a good feeling and returns so much to us in so many ways. Man really thrives on love! We need to feel love, receive love, and give love! If not there is a major void in our lives. Remember this is not just about people, it also about things. So a person may not have a partner to love, but loves their job, home, hobby, pet, or whatever, they are still in love. Love comes in so many ways which is one of the reasons why it's so hard to define in a simple manner. It is such a complex emotion, with so many variations and paths.

On the other hand, having a negative love experience is devastating. I don't want to dwell upon this type of love for long here in this book, because my objective is to focus on happiness. However, we must also deal with this negative side of things. Love, or the loss of love is probably the most devastating thing that can happen to a person, outside of serious illness. It truly emphasizes the true and massive, immeasurable value of this word and feeling. Losing a great love is earth shattering! Whether the loss comes in the form of death, divorce, health, job loss, misunderstanding, etc. it has more impact than any other event or episode that can occur in our lives. At this point, all I can offer is a few pointers that I gained through my own personal losses and hope that those of you reading this can get something out of it to help you move on.

The first thing I will say about coping is to first let yourself grieve. Whatever your circumstance, you will have to accept the loss and find a way to move forward. They say that the three most typical traumatic experiences that we can experience are loss of a loved one, loss of job, and divorce. At one point in my life I experienced all three in a four month period. I can tell you first hand that it all passes and you will survive.

Secondly, seek help from those close to you and if necessary professional help. During the timeframe of my losses, which I mentioned in the previous paragraph, I heard, saw, felt, and read so many things, including an overabundance of clichés'. I received so much advice, which simply passed from one ear to the other, that I wasn't really hearing anything and it meant nothing to me, consciously. But later I realized it was all having an impact on me, whether I understood it or not. I remember one of the things an older guy told me that sounded so stupid, but later on had real meaning to me. He said, "Remember they can kill you, but they can't eat you?" It wasn't until months later that I got the real message contained in the crude saying. For it meant that I always have the upper hand. Ha!

I can't offer you a magic bullet to get rid of the really bad and painful feelings that you may be experiencing, but I can offer you a few things to think about which I hope will help. One of the most prominent thoughts that sticks in my head from that whole experience was something someone said to me which went like this. "Keep looking ahead, you never know what's right around the corner! It could be the greatest and most wonderful thing that has ever happened in your life!" I grasped onto that saying and have always been grateful to whomever it was that told me that. The reason why it has such power in my thinking today is that it's true. Within two years of my devastating time, I met someone new who changed my life, and found the dream job of my life. Along with that came a new mentor, new friends, and world travel, everything beyond my wildest dreams. So I offer this saying to you and hope you will keep looking for that next corner or turn in the road which will change your life.

Another suggestion for you is simply what this book is all about. You must decide when you're done grieving, feeling bad for yourself, and want to change your feelings to something more positive. Of course, we can't stop our feelings immediately after something happens, but the course that those feelings take and how long we let ourselves be down is definitely our decision. Don't let yourself take too long!

So back to 'love and happiness'. So what is the message I want you to receive from this section? It is seek love! As is mentioned already, love comes in so many forms. You will need to find your passion, your wants, and your desires and then think, do, and take action to fulfill them. If you don't have a hobby, sport, or something that you love to do, besides sitting around, then get off of your butt and find something. I don't believe there is a normal functioning human being alive who can't find something to motivate themselves that they can love to do. It's a matter of looking. Sometimes, we have to go back in time and find something we used to do. I remember when I was a kid I worked at a golf course. I really liked trying to play golf, and I say "trying" because if you could see how I play you would agree. Early on in my career, after getting out of the navy, I tried playing again, but really became a little discouraged for several reasons, the main one being a lack of funds. So for about 15 years I didn't play the game. Then when my financial situation had changed and my career almost dictated that I play golf with clients and colleagues I picked the game up again. Today, I can honestly tell you, "I love playing golf with friends, strangers, or even by myself". Unfortunately, I haven't improved any, but who cares? Most of the time I don't even keep score. So find something that trips your trigger and get out there and do it. And by the way, there are many things that you can love to do that don't cost a lot or require anything special. I also discovered that I love to walk, so I walk around my neighborhood nearly every day. Costs nothing! I guess that explains why I like golf so much, a lot of walking. Someone famous once said, "Golf, a great way to ruin a good walk!"

I recommend that you create an "I Love" list. Take some time to list everything that you love and keep updating it. Keep the list around you and make it a priority to focus on the things on your list, particularly when anything gets you down. This is what is important in your life, not the other nonsense. Here are some examples from my own "I Love" list:

<u>I Love:</u>
My wife
To play golf
Writing
Reading
Travelling
My children and their families
My wife's family
My friends
Beer

Good wine
Crab Rangoon's
TGIF

This is just a short example of my list, it is actually much longer. Let this list be what you focus on and what inspires you. Of course, we still have to do many things we're not crazy about, but they should not remain in focus any longer than it takes to do them or confront them and get rid of them. "I love my 'Love List'!"

The Amazing Human Body

Sometimes we have things staring us right in the face that should make us incredibly happy, but for some reason until someone points it out, we never notice. Our bodies are one of those amazing things. The human body is the only machine in the world that never shuts 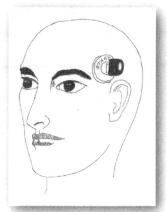 down completely. No maintenance shutdown, only reduction in operation. It shuts down only once, and that is at the end of our life. It is amazingly durable, dependable, and strong. We are very lucky to have such a magnificent machine to reside in and every day we should be grateful and happy. I want to share with you some of these amazing facts about our body.

The computer that controls this machine has two major modes of operation; conscious & sub-conscious. Conscious mode switches on and off, mainly during periods of sleep. Sub-conscious always operates in the background. An amazing control system with full computing capability and incredible multitasking functionality. We are only aware of a small fraction of our computers operations, because it is so highly automated. All basic body functions are regulated without any input from us. Breathing, heart pump, operation of valves, sensory input, safety systems, etc., are all automatic.

So here we are, owners of this incredible machine, which surpasses a Lexus, Maserati, Ferrari, the space shuttle, IBM computers, all the computers in the world, all science capability and more. At one point in my life I was teaching a weekly class at my church for the youth group. I used an analogy of how special we are and unique we are as human beings. I explained that if we were to gather all the scientists, engineers, computer specialists, mathematician, etc., etc. and had all the money and resources in the world we could not build a machine that could play one hole of golf. The decisions that have to be made and the actions taken are enormous if you really think about it. Just to highlight this process let me step you through what has to be done to play one hole of golf. First you have to decide to play. Then you must choose what to wear, what to take, decide where, how to get there, where to park, how to get your gear to the cart, pay, find the first tee, get ready, tee up the ball, chose a club, know which way to aim, hit the ball, go find the ball, chose another club, hit it again, and eventually when on the green, chose the putter, line up the putt and hit it with right aim and speed until it's in that 4"cup. Amazing! There is no computer in the world that can do that, but you are born with one in your head. Imagine that! And when you think about it, I have just given a rough overview of playing one hole of golf and there are eighteen holes on a golf course, and thousands of golf courses, and golf is just one of many sports and this is just a game. So do you grasp the power of our brain, this amazing computer?

And do we appreciate this privilege, this ownership? Not really! Especially when we complain. We say "oh, I don't have this or don't have that, life is so hard, I wish I had more, more, more, and so on and on, with wishes and complaints.

The point here is that we already have so much to be grateful for, built right into us and yet we never think about it or give ourselves a chance to feel good about it. As an engineer, I am constantly amazed about how my body works and how it continues to work for me. I am one lucky person and I am grateful for all I have, and you should feel the same way. We are surrounded by amazing things that if we take the time to think about them we can greatly affect our happiness and enjoyment in life.

We live in an age of such rapid technological advancement, that it is difficult to comprehend all that's around us. Yet with all this amazing science, technology and creative ability surrounding us we fail to recognize that our own bodies have a system that cannot be matched by anything or anyone in the world. Now, that makes me happy!

So we now know that we are the owners of this incredible machine, so we have to ask ourselves "are we using this machine to our full advantage, or is it parked in the garage most of the time?" When we think about happiness we must think what are the things that make us happy and how can the machine help us to do them. Pleasure, satisfaction, joy, success, accomplishment, just to name a few are all items that the machine is good at getting for us. But not unless we instruct it to move in the right direction, otherwise it remains parked. So I hope you can see the power that we have available to us and the fact that we have only to utilize it to our full advantage.

Let me use the writing of this book as an example of how this works. For many years I told myself that I wanted to write a book. I have dreamt about having a book and using it to create a show featuring a strong message that would impact and improve people's lives. Yet I only worked on it when I felt like it and I didn't recognize that the machine within me could help me make this book possible. I failed to turn on the machine! "Turning on the machine", in this instance, meant setting time aside and sitting down and writing. Sounds easy doesn't it? Nothing happened for long periods of time, until I told myself that I have to write a certain amount of words every day (500 words actually) if I wanted to get the book done. This clear, precise goal is what turned on the machine and magically the book got completed. All the knowledge, skills and information required to write this book were there within my reach, just waiting for me to turn the machine on and get them out into my manuscript. Once I did that, the book was done in a matter of months. Amazing!

The Horseshoe on the Beach

I grew up believing that 4 leaf clovers, a rabbit's foot, and horseshoes brought good luck. So when I was walking one particular morning at one of my favorite spots, American Memorial Park on Saipan, I came to a section in the park, where the wave action is washing away the island and has made some serious indentions in the shoreline, creating some unique lovely little secluded sections of beach. There in one such spot was lying a horseshoe! Probably got there as a result of someone playing the game horseshoes and then was just left there and disappeared under the surface of the ground. Now as part of the beach corrosion, it reappeared. It was really weathered and rusted from the saltwater and had some algae growth on it, pretty funky looking. But I picked it up and said, "Man is this good luck or what"? I brought it home and hung it on a nail at the back of my house, because I am convinced that something really good is going to come out of that. Some of my friend's think that's pretty wild and crazy, and quite frankly I don't blame them because not all people think like me. But you see, for me this is one of the secrets to finding happiness inside of ourselves. We must allow ourselves to dream, to be silly, to be crazy, and to think a rusty old horseshoe found on the beach could change our lives. You see, my thinking is if it doesn't work, so what? I at least had fun thinking it might work and enjoying those thoughts, which probably replaced something that would have been negative anyway. And by the way, a half hour after I hung up the horseshoe, I was chatting with a good friend of mine on the computer and he told me that hanging a horseshoe with the open end down is bad luck, so I ran out and turned it around. Thank goodness I didn't go anywhere during the 30 minutes it was hung the wrong way.

I also love to play the lottery! As a former engineer, with a pretty good background in math, I realize the possibility of winning is slim to nothing. But I still enjoy it and in fact when the lottery gets real big I generate an Excel Spreadsheet showing what I would do with the money. Oh my, you wouldn't believe how much fun I have with that document and dreaming about winning. When someone wins I remove the numbers and leave it in my computer in anticipation of the next money buildup. Do I get depressed when someone wins? Absolutely not, because I think of how happy they must be and how glad I am to have contributed to someone else's happiness.

When talking about lucky superstitions, I am always reminded of the many things my mother believed in. She was thoroughly convinced of many old German beliefs and the few I remember still stick with me. One is something I still do to this day. If I am walking on the street and I see a coin on the ground, I always follow my mom's direction. She believed if the coin is showing the tails side, you should turn it over to heads for the next person. If it is heads up you should pick it up and put it in your shoe for the rest of the day for good luck! Several times my wife has seen a coin fall out of my shoe at home while taking off my shoes and she looks really puzzled. I don't think she gets it, when I explain!

My mom also believed that if you turn a loaf of bread upside down on the table it will make the angels cry! Hmmm!

But don't get me wrong, I'm not suggesting you have to go out and do goofy things like that to be happy. But you must find something to put into the cavity in the top of your skull that is fun, positive, and helpful to your mental wellbeing, or you will never be happy. Think about that!

Opposites Attract

I would like to share with you a piece of my personal history and demonstrate the beauty of opposites meeting and attracting each other.

After years of working and living on the U.S. Mainland and suffering through a marital failure, I wound up living in the Mid Pacific in the Northern Mariana Islands on the island of Saipan, as I mentioned earlier. What brought me there was my youngest son, Jason, who has lived there for many years, working in the Marine Industry. So to cut to the chase, as I told you earlier, I was living a severely down-sized lifestyle, residing in a small room in the basement of someone else's house in the middle of the jungle. My income consisted of whatever I could generate as a substitute teacher, occasional seminar leader, and high school teacher and if I was really lucky an occasional consulting job. Many times I had no work so every morning I would walk for miles and miles on remote dirt roads or through the jungle, sometimes getting lost, but never worrying as it's hard to get too lost on a small island, because if you walk long enough you will eventually run into the ocean. During these walks I would contemplate my future and examine my past. After months and months of these quiet, uninterrupted, peaceful walks, I began wishing that I could meet someone who was uncomplicated, kind, honest and appreciated life as much as I did at this particular time. Incidentally, during this period I don't think I ever had one real date, nor pursued any women, as I was content just being alone. And so the story of meeting my wife unfolds and let me remind you again of what I said earlier, "You never know what's just around the corner".

On New Year's Day, I went to town for a late breakfast at a local restaurant and as usual I sat at the counter and enjoyed talking to the Thai and Filipina girls who worked there, most of them being good friends of my son and I. The place only had a few customers and it was very quiet and peaceful, as is typical on such a lovely island. Shortly after I arrived, a lovely mid-age Filipina came in and sat at one of the tables in the dining room. By her well-dressed but casual appearance, I assumed she was probably married to one of the Americans on island and I simply smiled as she walked by. I finished my breakfast and watched the TV behind the counter. Shortly the same lady appeared at the counter to pay her bill and was speaking to the waitresses, as they seemed to know her. At one point she asked the girls to call her a cab. She noticed me and politely said "hello". I was impressed with her demeanor and asked her where she was headed. She indicated she was going in the same direction that I was going and I offered her a ride, which she promptly declined. The girls immediately informed her that I was an ok guy and they had known my son and I for many years and it would be very appropriate and safe to take a ride with me. We were introduced properly and I met Flordelisa Jet Doctor. She accepted my ride and little did I know that this would be the luckiest day of my life!

On the way to her barracks, I informed Jet that I was planning to drive out to the northern end of the island and take in some of the wonderful scenery and tourist spots, which I had not visited for quite some time. I asked her to join me and she informed me that after 10 years on Saipan she had never had the opportunity to see this area. I was shocked, as the entire island of Saipan according to Wikipedia is only 12 miles long and 5.6 miles wide and I could not comprehend anyone living there for 10 years and never seeing the most scenic and beautiful part, which thousands of tourists travel to see each year. Of course, I forgot that Overseas Foreign Workers (OFW's), which is what she was, didn't have the same opportunities that the rest of us had. She never had a ride to take her there and quite frankly her life consisted of working at the main commercial laundry on the island, returning to her barracks, and going out dancing with her Filipino friends. So I convinced her to join me on this short trip and after she agreed, I stopped at a small store and bought a couple of cokes and some chips to snack on.

The afternoon was wonderful and Jet was so impressed with Suicide Cliff, The Grotto, Bird Island, Bonsai Cliff, and The Last Command Post, all major tourist attractions with spectacular views and scenery. Saipan is truly a magical place with its beautiful beaches protected by coral reefs, mountains, cliffs, plateaus, all filled with spectacular views and photo opportunities. The history of this and all of the Marianas Islands is so rich and interesting and the people are so kind, nice and accommodating. This is truly a place that makes it easy to get into the Static State, whenever you want. The beach BBQ's, cookouts, and great simple family and friend gatherings, where a nice cold beer tastes ever so good, is a welcome retreat from the world in general.

On the way back to take Jet home, I pulled into the former Nikko Hotel and took her to the pool bar, where she had a non-alcoholic tropical drink and I had my favorite, a cool Banana Daiquiri. The hotel staff was all inquisitive, as many of them knew Jet from her role as one of the people from the laundry who came there frequently to inventory the linens, etc. They also knew my son and I as frequent customers at the pool, bars, and restaurants. They were shocked to see the two of us together. Complete opposites by all definitions.

And so began a romance, which several years later wound up in a beautiful marriage, Jet becoming a U. S. Citizen, and I becoming one very, very happy husband. Our travels have taken us too many places for both business and pleasure and presently we spent our time living and working both on Saipan and in the Philippines, and operating a Training & Development company.

In looking at our differences and the benefits, it is not hard to identify them. Jet is good at managing money, applying absolute logic to all major decisions, and keeping things in there simplest forms. She likes to work at a regular job and make a contribution to our family. I enjoy doing some consulting and running our small training and development the company. I am semi-retired but welcome opportunities to contribute my knowledge and life experience whenever requested. I play lots of golf, enjoy laughing with my friends, and particularly enjoy seeing my son, daughter-in-law, and grandchildren on the island. If you're ever on Saipan and looking for me, I can usually be found at the beach bar.

Needless to say, this is a classic story of people coming from opposite sides of life and experiences, but finding the attraction to be overwhelming. I truly hope those of you reading this, who find your-selves looking for the right partner or situation, will take solace in my story and as I always tell people, "we never know what is right around the corner". I hope you will be as fortunate as I have been!

Influencers

Technology and Its Impact on Us

LATELY, I HAVE really started to pay specific attention to how much we are influenced and impacted by all the technology that has crept into our  daily lives. I realize at my age just how much the ability to live a simple life has been hampered by these things that are supposed to enhance our way of life. Certainly one cannot deny that this technology has streamlined the world and made so many things possible, easy to do, fast, convenient, and a multitude of other benefits that would take forever to list. Just a short while ago we believed none of this could ever be possible and we only saw signs of these developments in motion pictures or magazines, which really challenged our imaginations. Things like how our banking system works, record retention, communications, entertainment, medicine, and literally everything that touches us in one way or another. I am grateful for technology and at the same time I harbor many resentments about what it has done to our lives. In this section I want to point out some of the pros and cons this phenomenon has delivered into our daily lives. It is impossible to address every single aspect of technologies influence on us, so I will merely touch on a few areas as an example. So bear with me while I try to express my sentiments of this sometimes mystical thing "technology"! I also ask for your understanding with the fact that I grew up in a simpler era of history, before the real technological revolution, but later made a career as an engineer in the field of technology, primarily in the metals and aerospace fields. More importantly, I recommend that in the end, you should stop and take a look at what effect(s), both good and bad, technology has on your individual life and how understanding this can help to improve your happiness.

I will begin with one of my favorite subjects influenced heavily by technology, "Banking". For the younger people reading this book, this will be a lesson in history, which I hope you will enjoy. When I was a kid there was only one way to do banking! You had to go to the bank and talk to a human being. There was nothing you could do in banking without direct face to face communication with a live person. So it was cumbersome but very effective. It was slow and took time, patience and you had to go to the bank. If you had a problem you travelled to the bank and talked to a teller, representative, manager and explained your problem or need and they personally addressed those issues for you. Well, needless to say as the world population grew and more and more people were attracted to banking services, created by some clever and excellent marketing efforts, it became difficult for everyone to get the attention of a human being. Long lines at teller windows became frustrating for customers and banks learned quickly that this personal service cost a lot of money, so the idea was born along with the advent of computerization, that keeping people out of the bank was a practical and profitable solution for the banking industry. Moving ahead quickly, we changed from the human interaction to the machine interaction with the advent of the ATM and computers. So here we are in an era where you don't even have to go into a bank to open a bank account, because it can all be done online. Well, almost! It is important to note that with the advent of world security issues and the intervention of governments on personal lives and data, we became subject to the rules and regulation of agencies such as "Homeland Security". Therefore in most cases we have to show up in person at least once. With that said, we can conclude that the need to go to the bank really doesn't exist anymore. That's great for 99% of the time. Computers and their elaborate programs can do everything for us and the bank and it's wonderful! But wait! What happens when something goes even slightly wrong? How easy is it then? I just recently had a problem with my bank and was forced to communicate with them about a credit card that never arrived in the mail. I was out of my country and staying at my residence in another country, so it was not possible to visit a bank branch. So what were the methods of communication available to me? Well, that's simple, right? I could use their online messaging, which is found at my online account. That's how I told them my problem. Five days later they responded with a message that said my card had been blocked and cancelled. Ok with me as I didn't really want anyone else using my card. The message also said a new card with a new number would be mailed to my U.S. address. Along with the blocking of the card the computer also blocked my access to that card on my online account. Ever since I have had this card I made my payments and tracked my charges, etc. online and now it was all gone. The message I received from the bank about my new card being mailed, only contained the last four digits of the new card number. So now I can't see any activity on this card and I was simply waiting for the card to arrive in the mail to be forwarded to me at my present country location.

I will not bore you with the ensuing details of what happened in this situation, but will simply highlight some of the details of what happens when we step outside of that wonderful technology loop and outside of the computer program. Seven messages sent, with an average response time of 3-6 days, and always with the same message "Your previous card was blocked and new card ending in xxxx was issued". No matter what I wrote in the messages, no one really read them. Five phone calls to the banks 24/7 number from a foreign country to the U.S., with an average on hold time of 18 minutes, resulted in being told that the new card would be blocked and another new card would be mailed. When I inquired as to why I couldn't see the new card online, I was informed that the computer program requires that all my accounts that are shown online must have the same name on them and that my credit card has "SR" on it following my name and therefore needs to be changed by my visiting a branch. No matter how many times I told them that I never changed my name on anything, they simply could not respond, because the computer couldn't deal with that. So there I was, not having an active card for 7 months, no access to the account, no positive way to make a payment, and in total limbo. Eventually, after months of discussions it finally got resolved via a faxed letter to the bank changing my name, and the issuing of a new card.

Warning! Don't ever leave the perimeters of the computer program!

Information Overload

*"We live in a world where there
is more and more information,
and less and less meaning."*

FROM THE BOOK SIMULACRA AND
SIMULATION BY JEAN BAUDRILLARD

In today's world we are surrounded by a constant bombardment of information. I have always believed that too much of anything isn't good for any human being. Information overload can really cause some serious problems, which in most cases go unidentified. One of those problems is that this overload can grossly interfere with our ability to be happy, as we are too busy trying to process information rather than enjoying life. Everywhere we turn we are constantly subjected to information from so many sources and areas. This information comes in so many different forms, as it can be old, new, revolutionary, depressing, informing, etc., etc. It comes from social media, tv, radio, other people, billboards, everywhere! This information has become so predominant in our lives and it is nearly impossible to avoid or ignore, whether we like it or not! Man is not designed for this information overload and it is easy for us to become physically and mentally stressed by our outside world. Just like primitive man was challenged by nature and often shocked and threatened by animal attacks, neighboring clans, and nature itself, we are now subjected to the same levels of stress from far less obvious and visible sources, such as traffic, crime, climate change, wars, and of course information overload.

Our brains are programmed to want to process everything that we see, hear, feel, smell, and taste. So can you imagine how much data is input in a single minute, hour, day, week, month, or year? Little wonder why so many of us feel stressed and tired, but wonder why. Our processors are working 24/7! In fact, it has been proven that parts of our brains are much more active during periods of deep sleep, when the rejuvenation of our bodies is taking place. We force ourselves all of the time to seek answers by reading books, listening to professional speakers, constantly searching for magic bullets to help us relieve this stress. Yet all the time we're looking, we're taking in more and more and the overload continues.

So how do we deal with this condition? I don't think it is very difficult to learn how to shut-off the information faucet periodically and de-stress ourselves, but I do think it requires a better understanding of the problem, facing up to it, and certainly a great deal of discipline. Part of the problem is that we have been taught by the producers of information that we need to absorb all of it or we are weak! We develop fears and anxiety about not knowing.

The problem is that we live in a time when keeping us bombarded with information is a plus for commercialism, marketing, and governing. Flood our minds with more and more information and there is less processing time available to make sensible, quality decisions on all of life's important matters, including spending and saving. It is a known fact that people under duress spend more, eat more, sleep more, and waste more! So there's the motive of the "information overload movement".

If you want to face up to this issue you must reach some solid conclusions within yourself. First of all, let me tell you here and now, "you cannot know everything that comes your way and most of what you are bombarded with is meaningless!" The keyword here is "meaningless". I would suggest that you think about a few things that you have been bombarded with recently and then evaluate what they truly have to do with you personally. If you're honest with yourself you will discover that much of this information is meaningless and you could live perfectly fine without it. So you should see by now that what's happening is a deliberate flooding of your logical senses, via information overload. When you ride down the highway in your car think about how much information on those great looking billboards really has anything to do with you anyway. Of course, the good looking guys and girls are worth a second look, but what about the product or services. I can live just fine without that particular brand of jeans or shoes that super cholesterol laden burger, etc. So in fact if you look at all the billboards on just one trip to work or to the mall, ask yourself, "how much of all that stuff is really meaningful to me?" I try to focus on only things that I am interested in now. For example if there is a billboard for a place that I have been thinking about visiting, then I will look at it. But if it's a billboard for a place I'll never go to, I won't give it more than a glance and move on. I don't need that information! I think one of the coolest examples of this subject is a story I used to tell in my "Debt-Free & Prosperous Living" seminars. A guy was driving down the freeway in a convertible on the way home from the computer store. There is a box with a new computer in it sitting on the passenger seat next to him with the label, "Computer Model #22". As he's driving along he sees these guys putting up a billboard sign that reads "Introducing Model #23". What a shock! A great lesson on how we simply can't keep up with it all!

Computer scientists and development engineers are confronted with this same issue all of the time. Those who are on the leading edge of "Artificial Intelligence", particularly in the field of robotics, are just learning some simple lessons from those who have preceded them. An example is Polanyi's Paradox, Michael Polanyi, which says, "We know more than we can tell". Think about that!

So how do we shut down this information flow, when we decide we need to for our own wellbeing? How do we give our brain a break from the overload? First, you have to agree that at a specific time or period you do not want to have more information? You must consciously decide to limit the input or shut it down completely and then put yourself into a place where the information is not penetrating.

I find that just sitting somewhere peaceful with a glass of tea, wine, or a beer and concentrating on the view, taste, and general environment and refusing to let anything else is the simplest way of shutting off the information flow. Also, depending on the company, I find several of my friends can hold great discussions without having to introduce new information. Discussions about what did you do this week, the kids grades, what you love to do, usually don't require new information. So find ways to spend time in this mode and you'll really feel the reward from your "Information Break".

The Degradation of Emotional Communications

Let's talk now about how this technological revolution has affected our communications with each other. Oh yeah, I can sense you already see where this is going, coming from this old guy!

We are becoming more and more like robots. People agree to meet at Starbuck's and get caught up on things. But when I sit next to them I see everyone on their cell phone texting, talking,
reading, and doing everything except getting caught

up on things. They very seldom talk! It's so bizarre! I am tempted to ask them to put down their devices and talk for 20 minutes, but of course that would not be acceptable and very weird! I'm not saying that communicating via technology is bad and we shouldn't be doing it, but when it becomes an addiction we really need to step back and reconsider. Imagine that Priest's and Ministers have to tell their congregations to turn off their phones and not text in church! Physicians have to ask patients to turn things off when they are consulting them on their medical condition. This should never have to be necessary, simply out of respect for the person, place and time. Like everything else in this world there is a place and time for digital communications.

But the truth is that the loss of the ability to have face to face communications is a terrible one and there is an entire generation who don't understand what it really means to the well-being of relationships. We all know that when people really talk to each other face to face there are different kinds of communications taking place. There is of course the speaking of words and the choice of words but as important or even more important are the other forms of communications. I'm talking about "body language", 'tone of voice", "level of sound", "gestures", and "emotional content", all things which can never be transmitted over a device. When one fully appreciates these other methods of communications, it is hard to believe that we would attempt to do the majority of our communication without them. But unfortunately there is a generation of people who are so accustomed to the technology way, they don't even realize what's missing.

Again, I'm saying that we need to just plain talk to each other. I wish everyone could just set aside some time to have normal conversations with their families, friends and others. I find such pleasure in looking into the face of people I really like to talk to and see their expressions and reactions, and to feel their emotions and sense their responses to what I say or do. This feedback gives me such a vast array of information about what they are really thinking about themselves, about me, about what the topic is.

So I recommend that if you are not doing a lot of face to face communicating, try to do it and feel the true experience. I know that in many instances we can't do this, due to location, distance, time, etc. But where possible give a shot and take a "Technology Time Out".

Conclusions

It is my sincere hope that this book containing my thoughts, ideas, education, and most importantly personal experiences will serve as an inspiration and motivation to help you to find true success and happiness. I also hope that you will keep it near to you in your life's travels and that it will continue to serve you for a long, long time.

One of my major goals in life, in recent years, has been to touch the lives of as many people as possible in a productive and positive way so as to help them experience the true pleasure of being happy the majority of the time, as I have been so blessed to have experienced. There is nothing more rewarding or fulfilling than to know that others have benefitted, even in a small way, for one's own efforts, primarily through the sharing of knowledge and experience.

As you continue your journey in life keep the lessons and messages contained in this book near to your heart and practice them faithfully. Also, make sure you share them with your family, friends, colleagues, loved ones and everyone in general. If you meet someone who is temporarily unhappy, but genuinely looking to change, lend them you're new found wisdom and you too will experience the joy of knowing you have made a difference in someone else's life. Wishing you happiness and success and May God Bless You!

In closing, I want to share the following thoughts with you:

> *"The happiest of people don't*
> *necessarily have the best of*
> *everything; they just make the most of*
> *everything that comes their way."*

AUTHOR UNKNOWN!

"Happiness lies ahead for those who cry, those who hurt, those who have searched, and those who try... for only they can appreciate the importance of the people who have touched their lives."

AUTHOR UNKNOWN!

Author Biography

KEN SHANKWEILER, BORN in Allentown, Pennsylvania, was raised in a rural farming area. After serving one tour in the US Navy, he focused on higher education, obtaining degrees in psychology and electrical engineering. For the next thirty-five years, he worked in the corpo-  rate world, holding various positions at a number of Fortune 500 companies. Next, Dr. Ken (as he is called by clients and friends) toured the United States as a professional speaker with his own training and development company.

Shankweiler's company, Shankweiler Communications Consultancy, offers soft-skills seminars and professional speaking and consulting services in the Micronesia area, which includes the Philippines and Southeast Asia. He and his wife, Flordelisa, live on the Pacific island of Saipan, as does his son, Captain Jason Shankweiler, and his family. His daughter, Lisa Thomas, lives with her family in Virginia.

Shankweiler welcomes e-mail from readers and may be reached online through drkshankweiler@gmail.com.